PRINCESS TINA
BALLET BOOK·5

photographed by
mike davis

text: H. SHIRLEY LONG

850370 – 12 – 4

The very spirit of the ballet— Eva Evdokimova as Giselle

These young stars prove that ballet is

CONTENTS

© IPC Magazines Ltd. 1972   Book designed by James S. Green.

Published by IPC Magazines Ltd., Fleetway House, Farringdon Street, London, England. Sole Agents for Australia and New Zealand : Gordon & Gotch Ltd ; South Africa : Central News Agency Ltd ; Rhodesia and Zambia : Kingstons Ltd. Printed in England by Fleetway Printers, Gravesend.

a world of its own

THE great world of the dance, of ballet, knows no frontiers. Its beauty of movement, its music, its deep visual appeal touches chords in people all over the world. Race, nationality, creed, colour are of no account. The poetry of motion is in a language that can be comprehended anywhere. Ballet, in all its forms is in fact a world language on its own and the people who speak it come from dozens of countries.

Two of today's dancers illustrate this concept of ballet as a world language admirably. We show them on these pages. They are Eva Evdokimova and Cyril Atanassoff.

Truly international is Eva! She was born in Geneva, Switzerland, of parents who are Canadian and Bulgarian. She went to Munich, Germany, to study at the Munich Opera Ballet School and then on to London to our own Royal Ballet School.

Next step was to Copenhagen to join the Royal Danish Ballet in 1966 where she stayed three years and became a soloist.

While with the Danish Ballet Eva made her first British appearance since Ballet School days, in 1969, when she was a guest artiste in Leo Kersley's Harlow Ballet.

Underlining the international aspect of ballet, Kenneth MacMillan, then the British director of the Deutsche Opera Ballet in West Berlin, invited Eva to join his exciting company. In 1970 she competed in the big Varna International Festival of the Ballet in Bulgaria, which was apt for Eva! Against artists from all over the world Eva won a Gold Medal and through the international TV coverage a big reputation, particularly in Russia.

"Long-legged lyrical elegance" is how one writer described Eva . . .

The beauty of an arabesque by Eva Evdokimova

After this Eva teamed up with another new young international star, Cyril Atanassoff, from the Paris Opera Ballet, and they began to tour Europe. All stars come to London and in 1971 Eva and Cyril made their starring debut with the London Festival Ballet, first in Flower Festival at Genzano and then in the "test piece" of all ballet—Giselle.

Switzerland, Germany, Denmark, France, Britain—all countries are one to dancers like Eva Evdokimova and Cyril Atanassoff.

Three movements of ease and style by Eva partnered by Cyril Atanassoff in Giselle in London

Fresh, sincere, appealing . . .
that's Eva Evdokimova
in this movement in Giselle

Meet
Bertram Batell

WHEN it comes to appealing to each new generation the Ballet Rambert has a splendid attraction. They call it Bertram Batell's Sideshow. It all began a few seasons ago when the Rambert company, noted for its love of modern dancing and its experimental ballets, started some children's programmes in school holiday times and also in schools in term time.

They were a huge hit so the company developed them into what they called Bertram Batell's Sideshow, partly because they created a compere named Bertram Batell

and his fun ballet

who linked the items and in general presided over the goings-on. The Sideshow has a touch of the Monty Pythons about it!

Every season new items are added to the show and the whole thing is a Rambert Company enterprise; everybody does his or her bit in it. The pictures on these pages give you glimpses of ballets called Spandango, The Strong Man, Swerves and Curves with Sandra Craig, Joseph Scoglio, Gideon Avrahami, Mary Willis, Jonathan Taylor.

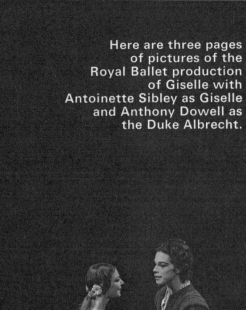

Giselle as Festival Princes
returns to her hom
in happy triumph

She is one of the most
famous characters in the
storyland of ballet–Giselle.
And it is not ungallant
to state that she is
about the oldest!
She was born in 1841 . . .

The shattered Gisel
pleads with Duke Albrech

Giselle has killed herse
on the Duke's swore

The romantic classic
ever young Giselle

GISELLE has come down to us almost unchanged since
the French poet and ballet expert Theophile Gautier
found himself fascinated by the German legend of the
wilis, those maidens who have died before their wedding day
and who come out of their graves at night in bridal dress to
dance until dawn. And should any man be caught in the wood
when the wilis are dancing, he is doomed to dance on and on
until he drops dead from exhaustion.

Gautier saw this as a great basis for a ballet, a romantic
theme of beautiful women, white gauze and moonlight. He
went to an opera librettist named V. de St-Georges, who turned
the bald theme into a play, and to a composer Adolphe Adam,
who wrote the music. The choreography was by Coralli and
the whole ballet was put together in a matter of weeks. Clearly
everybody was inspired, but those men could never have
dreamed that their work would live so long.

After all, it was a simple little story of the peasant girl who
falls in love with a man she supposes to be a peasant too, but
is the Duke Albrecht in disguise. When the peasant girl, who

was given the name Giselle, discovers his real identity and learns that he is to marry a princess she loses her mind and dies of grief.

A simple tragic tale much suited to the romantic mood of the eighteen forties. One of the foremost ballerinas of that day first danced the role of Giselle. She was Carlotta Grisi, an Italian.

The list of ballerinas who have danced the role since then is long and illustrious. It constitutes a kind of history of ballet down the last century and a half, for every dancer has brought to the role her own particular gifts and interpretation, her own style.

Consider these names: Pavlova, Spessiva, Markova, Karsavina, Alicia Alonso, Ulanova, Fonteyn, Grey, Shearer, Gilmour, Nerina, Beriosova, Page, Park, Anderton, Sibley, Wells, Samtsova. Those are the world stars who in this century alone have danced Giselle.

To dance Giselle with any success a dancer has to be very gifted technically, to be an actress, an artist, a personality. The reason why the ballet is not a quaint museum piece and has survived so brilliantly into a very different age is that the character of the peasant girl Giselle is genuine and her sufferings—in the art of a great dancer—move audiences to compassion.

When dancers talk about a classical ballet it is Giselle they point to as the supreme example. Romantic, classic ever-young Giselle.

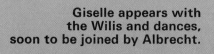

Giselle appears with
the Wilis and dances,
soon to be joined by Albrecht.

Star Portrait
MARGOT FONTEYN

...and here one of her

NO need to introduce her. She remains one of the great world figures of ballet, Dame Margot Fonteyn, CBE, Prima Ballerina Assoluta of the Royal Ballet at Covent Garden. Long has she reigned as "Queen of the Royal Ballet", as the Americans called her, but it comes as a slight shock to learn that it was 40 years ago that she first stepped on stage as one of the 32 snowflakes in The Nutcracker, an event which passed totally unnoticed.

You cannot really separate the career of Fonteyn from the rise and growth of Britain's National Ballet. She began with it at age 13 with the new Sadlers Wells School. And down the years she has played a vital part in making the dream of those pioneers Ninette de Valois and Frederick Ashton come true—a truly national British ballet with its own stars and style and values.

But all this was in a distant future when this dark-eyed young girl went for her audition to the Wells School in front of Ninette de Valois.

she dances greatest rôles

Discussing the hopefuls with her aides, Miss de Valois is reported to have said: "I like the look of the Chinese girl. Who is she?" The aides looked puzzled. Miss de Valois indicated the girl in question, and called her over. "What is your name?" "Peggie Hookham", replied the girl. "And where do you come from?" "Shanghai", replied little Miss Hookham. "There you are, what did I tell you, she comes from China", said the triumphant de Valois.

It was literally true that Peggie Hookham had not long arrived from Shanghai, where her Yorkshire father was a civil engineer and where she and her mother, who was of Irish-Brazilian blood, joined him. It was in Shanghai that Peggie had her first ballet lessons from an exiled Russian ballerina, Astafieva. Later she took her stage name from her mother's Latin-American family.

And for Margot Fonteyn, Freddie Ashton created some score of ballets one of which, Daphnis and Chloe, we show you here with Nureyev and others of the Royal Ballet.

15

Odette~Odile

the rôle that is every ballerina's ambition

THERE are many outstanding story characters in ballet. We've already met Giselle. Then there are Princess Aurora in The Sleeping Beauty; Swan-ilda in Coppelia; Petrushka; Ondine; The Firebird; Romeo and Juliet; Hamlet; The Miller and his wife in The Three Cornered Hat; Cinderella.

Although ballet is a team enterprise as a whole, it has its glittering star roles and in The Swan Lake we have the dual role of Odette-Odile. And that is the role every ballerina wants to dance. Most of the great ones have. In the ballet world they discuss the new young dancers and always somebody says "Ah, but wait until we see her in Swan Lake"

Top left: Anthony Dowell as Prince Siegfried: then (left to right) Antoinette Sibley as Odette-Odile, shown as Odile in the remaining pictures.

Left: Antoinette Sibley of the Royal Ballet as Odette in Swan Lake. The other pictures are of the ballroom scene at the Castle in act three when the drama unfolds.

Why is this? Like Giselle, Swan Lake is a true classical romantic ballet. The equally demanding leading role is, however, a little different. The emotions of Giselle call for depth of acting beyond conventional miming. Odette-Odile is really all dancing, and the miming has been curtailed of recent years.

Swan Lake is one of the oldest and still one of the most popular ballets round the world. Every company produces it and every dancer wants to be the heroine. Do you know the story? Odette is a beautiful girl who is transformed by a magician into a swan queen. Only at midnight for one brief hour can she resume her human form.

Act three is the highly dramatic sequence of events where the great Odette-Odile dual role emerges. Rothbart the evil magician who transformed Odette into a swan queen has a daughter Odile who is the very embodiment of evil, but she too is beautiful in her way. In act two we have seen that midnight hour by the swan lake when Odette returns to human form to dance. Prince Siegfried and his huntsmen come by. Odette pleads with the prince not to shoot her swans and in that moment he falls in love with her.

Act three is set in the lovely ballroom of Prince
Siegfried's castle to which his mother has invited some
young ladies as prospective brides for Siegfried, she
too being unaware of the true situation. And then the
dramatic moment when into the scene floats the figure
which Siegfried thinks is his Odette. She is Odile
transformed by her evil magician father into a replica
of Odette. Siegfried asks her to marry him, discovers
his mistake too late and runs from the castle.

Odette is beautiful and appealing. Odile is glittering, fascinating, wicked. Two widely different characters for the ballerina to dance. The dancing is brilliant
in this ballet. When it was created in 1877 by Petipa
with music by no less than the great Tchaikovsky, it
was strangely not a success. Revived seven years later
with the then great ballerina Legnani in the dual lead
it was a huge hit. It was Legnani who, as Odile,
introduced the now famous 32 fouettés, those pirou-
ettes on one leg in which the other foot makes a
whipping motion. It is still done but nobody counts
the fouettés now as they did in wonder then! And all
today's great dancers have danced the role: Fonteyn,
Beryl Grey, Moira Shearer, Rowena Jackson, Beriosova, Anya Linden, Antoinette Sibley, Doren Wells,
Monica Mason to name only a very few.

Anandavalli whom you see in three graceful poses here is a dancer of Ceylon. She travels the world performing the dances of her native country. She is now 21 years old and has been dancing since she was eight, her whole life is dedicated to showing the beauty of Bharata Natyam, which is the oldest dance form in India and one of the world's most ancient.

Anandavalli
DANCER FROM CEYLON IN HER COUNTRY'S MOST ANCIENT DANCES

Puppet who came to life...
The story behind PETROUCHKA

IT is one of the great story ballets, a "dance drama" we should call it now. By any standards it is a masterpiece of the art of ballet. If you wanted to show somebody quickly what ballet is all about, if you wanted to give them a glimpse of the history of the dance, then take them to Petrouchka.

It was first produced in 1911 but is still mounted by the world's ballet companies from time to time. For instance the Royal Ballet put it on, after a lapse of some years, at Covent Garden as one of the vehicles for the introduction of Rudolf Nureyev. He could not resist the lure of dancing the role of the puppet Petrouchka.

For that is what this most famous and classical ballet is about—the story of a puppet in a fairground. But Petrouchka is no sweet and sugary children's fairy story.

We give you three pages of brilliant pictures of the London Festival Ballet's Petrouchka . . .

The three main characters the Moor, the Dancer, Petrouchka . . . . Loggenburg, Samtsova, Prokovsky

The Magician brings the Dancer to life and she steps from the booth

He's called the Magician, the Sorcerer, or as Benois first named him the Charlatan: he is danced by Jean-Pierre Alban

The Dancer or the Doll is Galina Samtsova and the Moor is danced by Dudley Von Loggenburg, Festival Ballet stars

If you are newly come to the history and background of ballet I should explain that in 1911 there was a mighty force in the world of ballet named Diaghilev. He was the impresario, the presiding genius of the Russian Ballet at its prime. One of his composers was a young Russian little know then but world renowned now—Igor Stravinsky.

Stravinsky was working on a big composition for piano and orchestra, the basic idea of which was the picture of a puppet suddenly endowed with life and playing the piano, exasperating the orchestra with his wild notes cascading against the other instruments, who in turn retaliate until in a mighty crescendo of sound the poor puppet collapses. Stravinsky says he spent hours trying to find a title to express his piece until one day he "leaped for joy.

Petrouchka . . . the name of the puppet familiar on all Russian fairgrounds".

He played his piece to Diaghilev who was very intrigued by it and urged Stravinsky to turn it into a full ballet. The next man in the story is Alexandre Benois, the artist, who equally taken with the idea, drew the scenery from his own love of fairgrounds and created the role of the Charlatan, the Magician.

With a ballet shaping up they called in Michael Fokine, a young dancer who had become a wonderful choreographer. The music, the scenery, the story, costumes . . . and then the dances, the movements. But it *began* with the music, and the music became part of the action, not just an accompaniment. That is why Petrouchka is one of the "break-through" ballets, a turning point in the history of the dance.

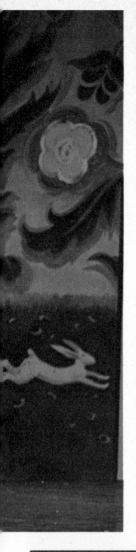

Petrouchka the tragic
puppet on the right is
danced by Andre
Prokovsky, another
Festival Ballet
luminary

The crowd in the old St
Petersburg fair ground
is made up of real
characters in the
brilliant choreography
of Fokine

23

Historic Originals

THE Nutcracker ballet, or to give its original title Caisse Noisette, is one of the most gay, colourful and visually exciting of the great classical works. Coupled with the flowing music by Tchaikovsky and the brilliant dances by Ivanov we have the costumes, and few ballets have so many varied ones.

Think of all those national dances in the scenes where little Clara is entertained in the Kingdom of the Sugarplum Fairy. There are Spanish dancers, Chinese, Arabian, Russian, there are harlequins, columbines and fairies.

The wonderful costumes in this work are the creations of one of the great men in the history of ballet—Alexandre Benois. He designed the costumes for such famous ballets as Petrouchka, which we have already seen, Les Sylphides and many more in the days when Diaghilev was master-minding the explosion of his Russian Ballet into the world outside Moscow and St. Petersburg.

Alexandre Benois was an artist, a critic who came of a family notable in the theatre.

Ballet is really team work and the artist-designer is vitally important. Costume and scenery designing is not merely a case of doing a few drawings for the wardrobe department or scenery builders. For ballet you must have an intimate knowledge of what a dancer needs. Benois had that expertness. He designed costumes a dancer could actually dance in! He knew that stage lighting often changes drawing board colours. He understood which materials were needed.

The six pictures on these pages are reproductions of actual drawings by Benois for the Nutcracker ballet in 1907. You can see his notes and instructions to the dressmakers. And though we can't show it he also pinned samples of the materials to his designs.

Beau Danube ~
The Viennese Waltz Ballet

A great ballet revived by the London Festival Ballet at a Royal Gala, Beau Danube with Strauss music and Massine choreography. Here are Dudley von Loggenburg as the Hussar and Shirley Grahame as the Street Dancer.

IT might seem an obvious idea to build a ballet round some of the world's most famous dance music. Especially with an almost equally ready-made setting. The waltzes of Johann Strauss and the city of Vienna in its heyday would seem to lie ready for the magic touch of a ballet creator. Oddly, only one outstanding ballet has ever been produced to use the lilting rhythms and melodies of Strauss, and that is Beau Danube. Its creator was one of the towering figures in the history of ballet—Leonide Massine, dancer and choreographer supreme.

It was a fine gesture when the London Festival Ballet celebrated its 21st birthday to stage Beau Danube again after a lapse of many years and to invite its originator to see it. Massine produced it and danced the lead in it as long ago as 1923, and there are some experts who say that only he can really interpret it . . . which is perhaps why we have not seen it of recent years. Beau Danube is truly the essence of Massine's art.

It is not a story ballet or a strictly classical one. It is in one act, has seven characters of which the Hussar is the focal point and in many revivals Massine danced the Hussar. Beau Danube's first stars were Lopokova, Marra and Massine; ten years later Danilova, Riabouchinska and again Massine dance it. The Festival Ballet's stars were Shirley Grahame, Margot Miklosy, Dagmar Kessler and Dudley von Loggenburg.

A characteristic lift by Dudley Von Loggenburg with Shirley Grahame in Massine's revived Beau Danube by the London Festival Ballet.

Beau Danube is full of amusing special dances, The Strong Man, Vassilie Trunoff, and the Street Dancer

The ballet is a sentimental tale but its characters are human and lovable. There are the two girls who love the Hussar, one timid and young, the other a bold street dancer. The other characters, realistic though they are, serve as pointers to the tale.

There are two dramatic ballet highlights. One is when the Hussar stands utterly motionless in the centre of the stage and reflects bitterly on his past while the other characters dance mockingly round him. It is said by people who saw him that Massine, just standing still in his gay hussar's uniform held the eyes of the whole audience, dominating the scene for a long time. The other highlight is when the Blue Danube is being played, the Hussar revives his love for the street dancer and he takes her in his arms.

Leonide Massine was a very young man when Diaghilev chose him to replace the genius Nijinsky when the latter left the Ballet Russe. In a very few years he was at the top. The list of his ballets is a history of the dance in modern times: The Three Cornered Hat, The Good Humoured Ladies, La Boutique Fantasque, La Symphonie Fantastique, and Beau Danube. When the Festival Ballet revived that, Massine himself was dancing to demonstrate his notation system with the Royal Ballet—in his seventies!

The crowd mocks the
Hussar, in the centre,
in a typical Massine
group effect

Pas de deux for the Hussar
and the Fiancee, Dagmar
Kessler, Dudley von
Loggenburg as the Hussar

Fiona McGregor, 12,
and on her points in
an attitude that shows
she is learning the
art of the dance and may
one day be a ballerina.

star protégé

FIONA IS 12 BUT SHE'S DANCING WITH THE STARS

FIONA McGREGOR like many thousands of girls wants to be a dancer, a ballet dancer, and like those thousands of other girls she knows that you have to train for it. So Fiona goes to class. She started ballet class at the age of 10, the approved age these days.

Fiona is the daughter of a well known Scottish TV ballad singer and she was enrolled with Anna Northcote. Now Miss Northcote is one of Britain's top professional teachers, many of the most famous names in ballet today have been her pupils. In ballet you never in fact cease to be a pupil, you are always in training, practising, rehearsing and always under the sharp eye of a teacher like Anna Northcote.

She operates at the London Dance Centre, which aptly enough is a ballet shoe throwaway from the Royal Opera House in Covent Garden. To it come many notable names in the dance, to join Anna's professional class, held regularly. And among these professional dancers you will see the tiny figure of Fiona McGregor. She's not there for fun and it isn't

Anna Northcote, one of London's leading teachers, talks to Fiona before class.

Belinda Wright, great ballerina, shows Fiona one of her own ballet costumes.

a gimmick. Fiona is learning fast and is keep-up with the professionals. They in turn are only too pleased to help and advise, and when we say that such stars as Belinda Wright and her partner Jelko Yuresha are regular attendants at Anna Northcote's professional class you will see that Fiona is in distinguished company. But there is no condescension in the attitude of those two world stars to the 12-year-old learner. In ballet everybody is a dancer and that is all that matters, it is a democracy of artists no matter what age or degree of fame. Fiona is not only learning to dance, she is learning professionalism.

The Dance Centre in Floral Street, Covent Garden, is a great place for a youngster wanting to get into ballet. It is the largest dancing school and centre of its kind in the world. Some 45 teachers attend and they have 150 classes a week. You can attend class with Belinda Wright, have lunch or coffee, buy the latest book on ballet, rehearse, find engagements, buy ballet shoes and costumes and shoot a film there, all under one roof. Only a few years ago when its founder Gary Cockrell took it on, it was a disused Covent Garden market fruit warehouse.

And to refresh your memory: Belinda Wright is one of this country's leading dancers, who has appeared all over the world with the Ballet Rambert, The Royal Ballet and the London Festival Ballet, in recent years with Jelko Yuresha as her star partner.

In ballet class there is always a teacher with a keen eye and strong control who supervises your every movement and makes you do them over and over again until they are right. Fiona McGregor knows this routine well. But in these pictures she has the assistance of Jelko Yuresha, one of the leading male dancers of today.

Are You Learning To Dance?

You have just read of the training of one young dancer. Now turn to page 38 of this book for three pages of instruction in pictures on the basic positions and movements of ballet, demonstated by ballerina Jacqueline Tallis, and three pages about a famous Ballet School.

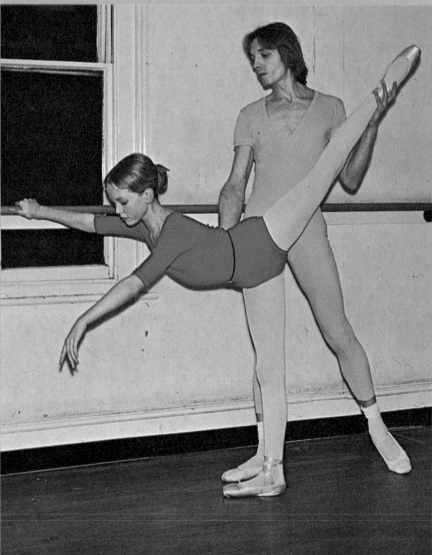

Flamenco!

The Thrilling Gipsy Dance of Spain

They call the Fiesta Gitana da Silva ''an explosion of wild gipsy dance''. This is a grand company of Flamenco artists gathered from all over Spain, with new members every year, artists who keep alive the true gipsy music, dance and song and tour round the world with pride.

On these two pages and the preceding ones we show
you colour action pictures of the Fiesta Gitana
company in action on their last London visit. They
danced Fandangos from Andalusia; tangos from
Malaga; caracoles from Cadiz; Bulerias, the
calypso song and dance of Flamenco; the Martinette,
the hammer rhythm working song of the gipsies;
and the Cuadro Flamenco, the group folk songs.

A typical shot of Isabel Romero, leading woman dancer, in the heel clicking rhythm of the fandango. Her costume is a gorgeous traditional one which sways to the rhythm of the guitar and castanets.

Leading dancer of Fiesta Gitana is Curro Velez; leading woman dancers are Curra Jiminez and Isabel Romero; leading singer-dancer La Pelua.

The sharp very strong and rhythmic hand clapping is typical of all flamenco music and dance and the whole company joins in it. There are 20 singers, dancers and guitarists in the Da Silver troupe and Curro Velez is the choreographer for the big exciting production dances.

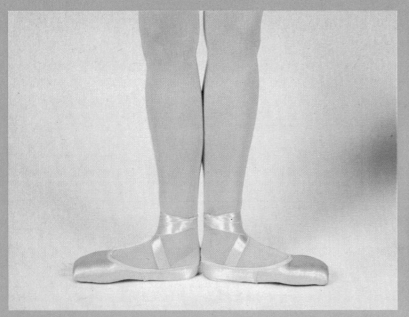

This is the first
position of the feet

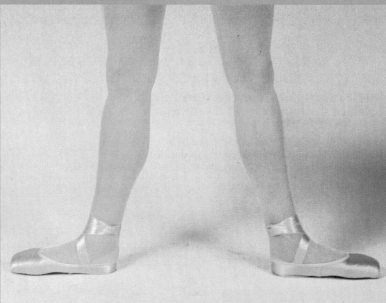

The second position,
feet apart in an "open
position"

ALL BALLET BEGINS

Jacqueline Tallis, ballerina,
working at the barre in a
practice leotard,
on a beautiful position known as
"développé croisée devant". You
need to be supple to raise your legs
like that . . . .

WHEN you are watching a major ballet company, the Royal, say, or the Festival or the Rambert, it is difficult, seeing all that poetry of motion, all that graceful elegant athleticism, to realise that it all begins with the human legs and feet in just five basic positions!

For all those great dancers—Fonteyn, Nureyev, Antoinette Sibley, Anthony Dowell, Svetlana Beriosova, Belinda Wright, Doreen Wells, Samtsova, Verdy, to name only a few, began their careers as children learning the five positions, of feet and arms, but first the feet.

Think of the beautiful edifice that has been built on those simple foundations, the steps, the movements of arms and body, the leaps, glides, walks and runs. A whole international language has evolved down the years, the language of motion, of the dance which can express emotions, tell stories and create atmospheres.

We show you those five basic positions of a dancer's feet on these pages and some of the beautiful movements and positions that have developed from them. But of course the progress from one to the other takes years of hard work and practice, practice, practice! The names of those positions and movements are in French, for although ballet is world

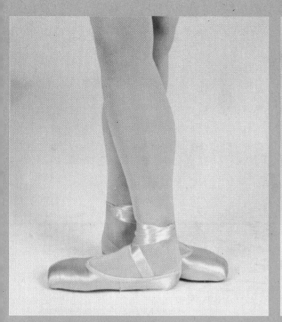

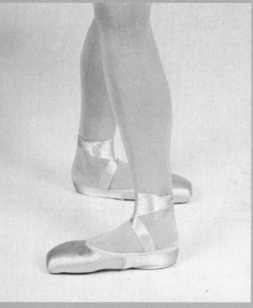

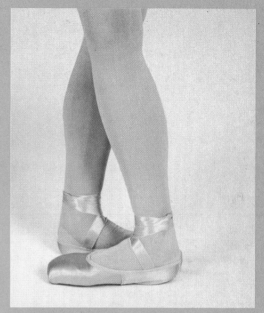

The third position is a "closed" one, feet touching

Position four of the feet is also an open one

The fifth position with feet touching

WITH THIS !

The Five Positions of the feet

wide and is a language of its own, its technical terms are always in French. The reason is that all ballet training is really based on a standard of rules evolved from the Academy of Dance established in Paris by King Louis XIV in 1661. Had they been able to film those early ballets you would see very great differences compared with the ballet of today, but it is still true that the basic vocabulary of steps and movements was laid down in French then. The use of French also provides a universal technical language for dancers, an international code that they all understand. Which is why you can gather together dancers from half a dozen countries and when it comes to carrying out the ballet master's instructions everybody knows what to do. When the choreographer says that he wants a pirouette, or an arabesque or a grand jeté, the dancers know exactly what he means.

Another branch of the language of ballet is mime and that too is international. There are a couple of dozen recognised gestures and movements used for the most part in the older classical ballets which have exact meanings and are part of a dancer's basic training, no matter what kind of dancing he may go on to. You can recognise some of them very easily. For example to express LOVE the dancer holds both

Jacqueline Tallis shows how a trained ballerina uses the barre of a studio to achieve "line" and sureness of position in that 90 degree angle of the leg outstretched in an "attitude effacé"

hands over the heart. To say I the dancer points towards himself with the middle fingers of both hands. For YOU he points to the other person with an open hand. For a KISS the lips are touched with a finger. So you see the language of love is basic in ballet!

Many ballet mime gestures are in everyday use by all of us: to say stop in mime you hold up the hand palm out in a strong gesture. Anger is expressed by raising the arms above the head with the elbows to the front and shaking the fists. That's almost the cliché expression of rage in plays and films, isn't it?

But all this comes later in a dancer's education. Everything really begins with the five positions of the feet, an exercise often begun at what is called the Barre, which is simply a bar or rail attached to one long wall of a school room or studio. Pupils can hold on to the barre in those nervous early stages and they learn to touch it or hold it lightly, not grasp it! Then when the positions of legs and arms are properly learned they have to be done in the full class away from the barre in what is called centre practice.

Interesting to think that these beautiful elegant arabesques of a ballerina began at the barre. That is where all grace, suppleness and ease is acquired. All the principles of ballet movement are based on the plié or knee-bend and the "turnout" of the legs from the hip, at an angle of ninety degrees. All beginning with the five positions of the feet and the arms. Every movement in ballet starts and ends in one of the basic five foot positions—"closed position": feet touch. "Open positions": feet parted.

The basic arms positions are hands gently clasped in front at waist level; arms outstretched each side at shoulder level; the right at shoulder level with the left upraised in a gentle curve; the right arm back to its first position with the left raised; and both arms raised upright above the shoulders.

One of the questions you often hear discussed is "at what age should you start to learn ballet dancing?" The experts say it should not be studied before the age of eight: nine or ten is not too late to begin either. Toe work "on the points" should never be attempted before the age of ten and then only after three years of study under a proper teacher of ballet. To many people ballet is mainly toe dancing; all they can see is the dancer "sur les pointes". But ballet is very, very much more than that! Did you know that it was only about 150 years ago that dancing on the points came into use? The Italian ballerina Taglioni first did it and caused a sensation.

Now in classical tutu on the stage Jacqueline Tallis demonstrates a flowing arabesque

One of the loveliest lines in ballet is expressed by Jacqueline in this "attitude croisée"

BALLET'S YOUNG GENERATION

The company assembles on the stage of
the Adeline Genée Theatre for
a Bush Davies special performance

THE ballet, the world of the dance, will never wither away for lack of new young blood and fresh eager talents. And there has never been a time when more opportunities are open to the new young blood. One of the most significant developments in British education of the past thirty years or so has been the growth of schools for arts education, schools where training in all the theatre arts, ballet, acting, music is combined with first class grammar school ordinary schooling. There are more than 500 such schools and you could spend your entire school life from five to fifteen at any of the major ones.

The local dancing school has come a long way! And one of the people who have done much to bring about this forward surge is Noreen Bush, one of the leading figures in British ballet education. Her whole life has been devoted to ballet. Nearly 60 years ago her mother opened a dancing academy in Nottingham and Noreen in due course joined her in it. In 1930 she married

The programme gives a chance
to the very youngest students at Bush
Davies School

Entrechats are far away, this is O-Level work in a school classroom

A beautiful classical ballet group by four senior girls at the Adeline Genée show

(Centre) The dorms of schoolgirl stories were never like this one at Charters Towers!

Maybe half a school working day is spent practising at the barre

Victor Leopold and together they built up the local dancing academy into a powerful educational force. In 1939 they linked up with one of their own old students, Marjorie Davies, to form the Bush Davies Schools, with a day vocational school at Romford, Essex, and a boarding school named Charters Towers near East Grinstead, in Sussex. This was one of the first schools of its type to be recognised as efficient by the Department of Education and Science, in 1953. At Charters Towers you can get your GCE O Levels and a full ballet training.

The East Grinstead school has also a splendid theatre of its own, not just a school theatre but a fully equipped professional playhouse, situated in the estate. It is called The Adeline Genée Theatre and there is a story attached to that.

Group scene in a ballet for all ages
called Christmas Eve in a
Czechoslovak Village

Everybody gives a hand with the
stage costumes which are created and
made in the school

Adeline Genée was a leading ballerina of the Edwardian days in London but more than that she did great work for the furtherance of ballet. She was one of the little group of enthusiasts who founded the Royal Academy of Dancing some fifty years ago and helped to raise the standards of teaching with their certificates. Noreen Bush was one of the first five dancers to pass the first advanced level examinations of the RAD and the very first winner of the Solo Seal. Noreen Bush became the friend and colleague of Adeline Genée and to keep her memory green in the world of ballet for which she did so much, Noreen inspired the building of the Adeline Genée Theatre as part of the Bush Davies School at East Grinstead. The pictures you see here were taken at the school.

(Centre) Scene from The Emperor's New
Clothes based on the Andersen story

Learning to achieve line and grace
under the eye of a ballet teacher

MACBETH

THE plays of Shakespeare are compounded of words; poetry, with drama and action, too, but we always think first of those wonderful words. Which is why there are few ballet or dance drama versions of Shakespeare; only Hamlet and Romeo and Juliet spring to mind. But in 1970 Edward Gaillard the man who runs that splendid "grass roots" dance enterprise Ballets Minerva realised an ambition he had nursed for years—a ballet version of Macbeth. It took him a long time and much thought and work but he succeeded in putting together a dance drama based on the play, containing all its essential highlights, in one act and a running time of 35 minutes.

In it he shows Death coming to claim Macbeth who lies mortally wounded in combat. Visions of those he has

murdered arise before Macbeth's eyes and in his last few seconds he relives those fatal events that have brought him to his end.

The characters are Lady Macbeth, Macbeth himself, Banquo and Duncan and the three witches, who are depicted with masks and stylised costumes. Death, too, is a masked character in an effective costume. The whole production is simple but vivid. Edward Gaillard adapted the play and did the choreography. The music is from various overtures and pieces of Berlioz, again adapted and arranged by Gaillard. The Minerva Ballet have been doing this ballet in schools with terrific success: Shakespeare in ballet is strong dramatic stuff!

Lady Macbeth is Kathleen Gray, who designed the costumes; Macbeth is Roy Morton; the three witches Morag Anderson, Colly Northwood, Ceris Vivian; Death is danced by Margaret Cameron, Banquo by Frank Weekes, Duncan by Harold Foster

WITHOUT WORDS

Shakespeare's play has been created in ballet by Edward Gaillard and the Minerva Ballet Company

BURMESE DANCING
Is Unique and Beautiful

THE beauty and fascination of the national dancing of Burma has been known to travellers for a long time but few people in the West have ever been privileged to see it. So when a big company of Burmese national dancers and musicians came to Britain last season Mike Davies was there with his colour camera to record it.

Burmese dancing dates back some 12 centuries and in its life has been influenced by the cultures of the Hindus, Siamese and Chinese. The dancing portrays the manners and customs of the old Imperial court, the life of the villages and some classical Buddhist tales. The music is most interesting, with drums, gongs, clappers and cymbals producing the sound. The players sit in little circular highly decorated enclosures with all their instruments round them, as in the picture bottom right.

ROYAL GALA HIGHLIGHT

You could call these next three pages a grand showcase of ballet! The ten super colour pictures demonstrate ballet at its best by top international artists. This is not the thing you would expect to see on an ordinary visit to the theatre, even to a night by a major company. These action photographs were shot at a special occasion, a birthday celebration by the famous London Festival Ballet. Guests in the audience included members of the Royal Family, several of whom are keen supporters of the ballet, Princess Margaret in particular.

If the audience was royal so was the list of dancers, for many of the princes and princesses of the kingdom of ballet appeared: Violette Verdy and Edward Villella from the great New York City Ballet; the Festival Ballet's own Galina Samtsova, Andre Prokovsky and Dudley von Loggenburg; Liliana Cosi from La Scala Ballet, Milan; Patrice Bart from the Paris Opera Ballet; Eva Evdokimova and Cyril Atanassoff from the West Berlin Opera Ballet and the Paris Opera Ballet respectively. Glittering and star-studded are the words that spring to mind! On an occasion like this the dances and specialities to be performed are chosen for their brilliance and effectiveness, they are truly showpieces to display the best of the talents gathered together.

Violette Verdy and Edward Villella from the New York City Ballet chose a most interesting piece. It was described as the Tchaikovsky Pas-de-deux. Its story is this: when The Swan Lake was first produced in Russia in 1877 it was, astonishingly enough, not a success! The score by Tchaikovsky was put aside. When eight years later the ballet was staged afresh it was a huge success and has remained so to this day. But one or two pieces of Tchaikovsky's music were lost in the new production. One in particular lay among his papers for many years until it found its way to Georges Balanchine, who was the mighty Diaghilev's last choreographer and went on to found the New York City Ballet.

He did the choreography for a spectacular pas-de-deux for Violette Verdy of his own New York troupe, which she now dances at special occasions with Villella.

Another spectacular pas-de-deux is the Black Swan dance from The Swan Lake, with Odile in the black tutu traditionally worn for the role. This was the choice of Liliana Cosi and Patrice Bart.

So if you study these three pages you will have an idea of the grace, elegance and beauty of line shown by stars in the pas-de-deux. You will see arabesques, attitudes, holds, and leaps, and you will see how the modern male leading dancer supports the ballerina in every way.

ALVIN AILEY
Artistry

It is not a ballet company in the sense that we refer to the Rambert or the Royal. Alvin Ailey calls his company the American Dance Theatre. It has been called the best in American negro dancing. The company has no stars or ballerinas as such, but is just a group of dancers. But what dancers! One eminent British ballet critic wrote of them "The company danced like people possessed, but possessed of a great and glorious vision in which they wholly believed". An American critic said "The Ailey dancers probably have more popular and universal appeal than almost any modern company you can name".

Alvin Ailey is their leader and chief choreographer and a feature of his work is his use of traditional negro folk music and such composers as Duke Ellington, Miles Davis and "Cannonball" Adderley, the jazz men, and our own George Harrison. Our pictures show items from their Child of the Earth and Steams ballets, taken on their last London visit.

Norman McDowell and Carol Grant.

DRESSING THE DANCERS

WHEN we are in the audience at the ballet we often say "Oh, what lovely costumes". The reaction of a dancer when shown a new costume or designs for one is "Oh lovely—but shall I be able to dance in it?"

A very important difference! In any type of ballet or dance production the costume is virtually a physical part of a dancer. He or she has to move in it, swiftly sometimes almost violently and costume and dancer must never part company! Nor must dancing clothes ever get in the way of the action. Imagine a ballerina wearing a plumed head-dress that tickled her partner's nose, or got caught up in the scenery. Or a costume with a waist or hip decoration that made it awkward for the dancer to be lifted by her partner.

On these pages we meet a man who certainly fulfils that requirement. He is Norman McDowell who was a dancer of distinction with several of the

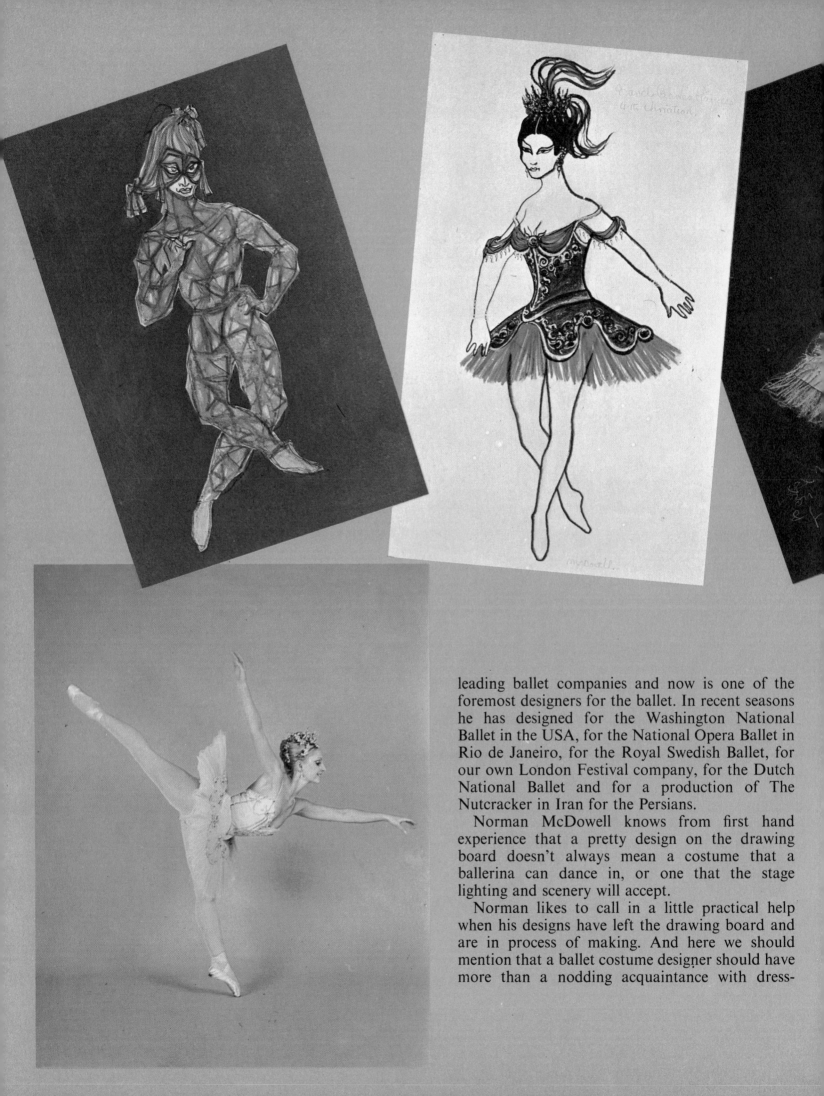

leading ballet companies and now is one of the foremost designers for the ballet. In recent seasons he has designed for the Washington National Ballet in the USA, for the National Opera Ballet in Rio de Janeiro, for the Royal Swedish Ballet, for our own London Festival company, for the Dutch National Ballet and for a production of The Nutcracker in Iran for the Persians.

Norman McDowell knows from first hand experience that a pretty design on the drawing board doesn't always mean a costume that a ballerina can dance in, or one that the stage lighting and scenery will accept.

Norman likes to call in a little practical help when his designs have left the drawing board and are in process of making. And here we should mention that a ballet costume designer should have more than a nodding acquaintance with dress-

making. He must know about materials and how they will make up for a dancer and the stage.

Our pictures show Norman with dancer Carol Grant from the London Festival Ballet. She had worn his costumes on the stage but says that she has never lost her childhood passion for dressing up and when Norman invited her to model some of his designs for us she couldn't resist the fun of trying on new clothes.

So on these pages you will see Norman McDowell's sketches for the costumes of the Ugly Sisters and a ballroom guest in Cinderella; two for Harlequinade; while Carol models a Sugar Plum Fairy costume and a Pas Deux Romantique of the Festival Ballet.

Norman told us that tights were invented in the late 18th century in France and the tutu, the flowing knee length dress in Italy much later.

The cast in our pictures is as follows with the colour of their leotards identifying them:—

Laura Connor	blue
Ann Jenner	pink
Monoca Mason	apricot
Lynn Seymour	green
Antoinette Sibley	mauve
Michael Coleman	salmon
Anthony Dowell	gold
Jonathan Kelly	mauve
Rudolf Nureyev	brown
David Wall	green

Dances at a Gathering

THE pictures on these next five pages may well be historic! Photographer Mike Davis went to a rehearsal of a brand new ballet going into the Royal Ballet's repertoire at Covent Garden. It was a creation of Jerome Robbins called Dances at a Gathering.

In the world of modern dance Jerome Robbins is a name to conjure with and this was his first new ballet for ten years. Robbins was the man who did the choreography for West Side Story, both original New York and London stage productions and the Hollywood film. And West Side Story was a major break-through in dance drama, a landmark.

Robbins had made his name in ballet originally with Fancy Free, where he teamed with composer Leonard Bernstein in a modern ballet about three American sailors on shore leave. Here was a ballet full of slapstick humour and brilliant dancing.

And now Jerome Robbins was back to the stage with Dances at a Gathering, created for the New York City Ballet and brought naturally to Covent Garden. This was not at all like Fancy Free or West Side Story. Jerome had gone back to pure classical ballet. No story, no drama, just dancing, with wonderful music by Chopin played on one piano, simple classical costumes, marvellous lighting. It was a magical mixture of theatre and on-the-points ballet.

In some performances the following Royal Ballet members dance; Lesley Collier, Alfreda Thorogood, Jennifer Penney, Marguerite Porter, David Ashmole, Donald MacLeary, Carl Myers.

The dances were in a way a linked series of exhibitions, of solos, pas de deux, pas de trois. The music consisted of eight Chopin mazurkas, five waltzes, three etudes, a scherzo and a nocturne.

In the final public production we saw the costumes designed by Joe Eula who is a notable fashion artist well known at the Paris collections.

Dances at A Gathering lasts just over an hour. The ten dancers, five men and five women, reflect the varying moods of the Chopin music, the dances are funny, sad, spectacular, heroic, amorous. There is no corps de ballet and one sees the ten dancers together only when they come on at the end to take their bows. One ballet critic has called this "as perfect a work of art as I have ever seen on the ballet stage".

Here's a typical scene from a London Contemporary Dance Theatre production at The Place, the home of modern dance in London, with more pictures on the next two pages . . . .

THE BALLET OF TODAY

IF you meet a fellow ballet lover and she says "Let's go to The Place and see what they are doing there", you must resist the natural question "What place?" and just go along with her to what was once a Territorial Army drill hall and HQ in Duke's Road which is just by London's Euston Station. An unlikely place you might think. But in the past few years that military looking building has become one of the most stimulating and interesting centres for the dance and its allied arts in this country.

The Place *is* its name! Inside you will find a fine small theatre, rehearsal studios, restaurant and bar and a casual friendly atmosphere. The usherettes and waitresses are dance students and you will find dancers all around you, for mainly The Place is the home of the London School of Contemporary Dance. And if you want to learn what modern contemporary ballet is all about there's where you will find it. It is young, daring and international. There are upwards of 60 regular students and 150 part-timers including teenagers and children. The Arts Council of Great Britain, the Gulbenkian Foundation, the London Borough of Camden and the Inner London Education Authority are all supporters of it. The artistic director is Robert Cohan who had a distinguished career as dancer, choreographer and teacher in America and Israel, notably with the famous Martha Graham Company. He is now principal choreographer and ballet creator for The Place.

On these two pages are special moments from four London Contemporary Dance Theatre ballets, Cell, Divertisements in the Playground of the Zodiac, Consolation of the Rising Moon, Cantabile

The dancers are Robert North, Xenia Hriba, Barry Moreland, Linda Gibbs, Franca Telesio, Micha Bergese, Norman Murray, Paula Lansley, Clare Duncan, Bob Smith, Irene Dilks, Micheline McKnight, William Louther, Celeste Dandeker, Noemi Lapzeson

The choreography for these ballets is by Robert Cohan, Noemi Lapzeson, and William Louther. The designers are Peter Farmer, Norberto Chiesa, Peter Docherty

The rats have gone and the children play in Hamelin

The piper's tune begins its work as the rats gather

The Pied Piper

BECAUSE of their simplicity and their visual appeal the great stories for children are a rich field for ballet creators. In the classic world we have Cinderella, The Sleeping Beauty, Peter and the Wolf all done by the famous companies.

That notable "grass roots" ballet company Ballet Minerva, whose policy is to take the joys of ballet to the places where people have little chance of seeing it, has a fine record in producing ballets from children's stories. They have done Alice in Wonderland, Hansel and Gretel, The Wizard of Oz and most recently The Pied Piper of Hamelin, a story that cries out for dance treatment.

The Pied Piper (Kathleen Gray) starts to lure the rats away

Scene from the finale Children's
Land where all ends happily

The White Rat is Suzanne Sarova who
later dances the little boy left behind

Takes The Stage

Minerva director Edward Gaillard and ballerina Kathleen Gray took the classic story and made it into a two act ballet. Kathleen Gray danced the character role of the Pied Piper and a dozen members of Minerva danced all the other parts of burghers, rats, Mayor, boys and girls and children. And this handful of dancers succeeded in peopling the stage with the characters of the little town of Hamelin as the Robert Browning story came to life in terms of the dance.

The music is taken from the work of the Italian composer Rossini. Costumes, lighting, scenery came from Edward Gaillard and his band of enthusiasts.

The mayor refuses to pay
the agreed thousand guilders

BALLET OF THE FUTURE

It has been called way-out, bizarre, futuristic. It has also equally been called breathtaking, imaginative, beautiful. We have had modern ballet and a step further forward to contemporary ballet, but the only thing you can call the Dance Theatre of Alwin Nikolais is the ballet of the future.

Alwin Nikolais has been a leader on the modern dance scene for some 16 years and he is still unique and successful. What is the essence of his Dance Theatre? He seems to throw aside all the accepted ideas of ballet to paint pictures using living moving figures against backgrounds of vivid flowing colour. He uses masks, props, mobiles, costumes, scenery to create a continuously flowing series of shapes and designs. It is a magic box entertainment, an art form that anybody can understand and enjoy. It is dazzlingly theatrical—and fun. And as the BBC has shown the Nikolais concept of ballet and theatre goes splendidly on the small colour screen.

Alwin Nikolais is himself responsible for the choreography, the sound scores recorded on stereophonic tape, the costumes, the lighting designs and the backgrounds. He has a troupe of 12 young dancers who carry out his exciting creations with brilliant skill.

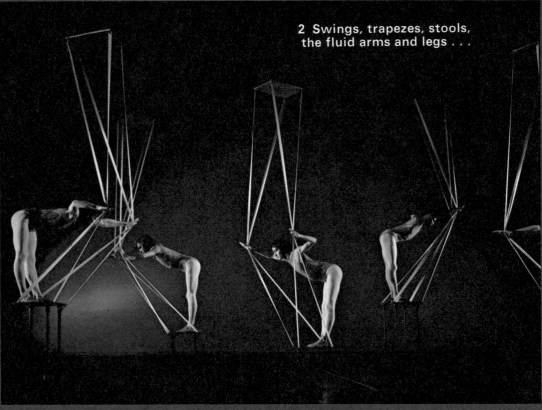

2 Swings, trapezes, stools, the fluid arms and legs . . .

1 No storylines or drama in an Alwyn Nikolais ballet, just colour and line and movement

3 of four brilliant and graceful dancers . . .

4 plus simple lighting and that's a Nikolais ballet!

8 They would call this a pas-de-trois
in the world of classical ballet!
It is Trio from Imago in the
Nikolais Theatre programme and it is
typical of how he gets his effects,
this time a gay funny one, but with
colour and shape still supreme

9 These costumes by Alwin Nikolais may
look impossible to dance in, but they are
very much a part of the choreography,
swinging and swaying with the legs
and arms of the dancers to form almost
a dance of their own in an oddly amusing
concertina-like way

7

5 The shapes of the dancers' bodies, long coloured streamers and subtle lighting against a dark background . . .

6 The dancers move in intricate patterns using the streamers almost as maypole dancers did, to create a flowing elegant series of geometric designs

7 This kind of ballet demands precise control split-second timing and immense concentration from the young dancers of the Alwyn Nikolais Dance Theatre

10

11

10 There's a touch of the flamenco dancer's costume about the way these costumes swing. Now here are the names of the dancers in the Alwyn Nikolais company seen on these two pages of pictures taken on their last visit to London from America. . . .

11 Carolyn Carlson, Emery Hermans, Tandy Beal, Bob Beswick, Rick Biles, Kathleen Gaskin, Suzanne McDermid, Claudia Melrose, Gerald Otte, Wanda Pruska, Robert Soloman, James Teeters

WE END WITH
IN THE BEGINNING!

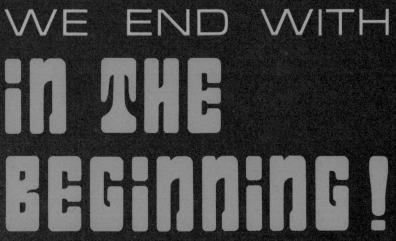

In ballet you can never stand still —in more senses than one! And the Royal Ballet knows that, which is why they encourage their young choreographers and musicians and have formed an experimental group. From it has emerged Geoffrey Cauley, a RB dancer for 10 years, who has turned choreographer. The first of his ballets to be given a public performance by a professional group was In The Beginning.

It is the Genesis story, the Garden of Eden story. Adam and Eve are danced by David Wall and his real life wife Alfreda Thorogood. The tempters are danced by Lucette Aldous and Hendrik Davel. Music is by Poulenc and decor by Peter Unsworth.

Here we see Alfreda Thorogood and her partner David Wall, two of the most promising dancers of the Royal Ballet today.

partnership of Alfreda Thorogood
David Wall started
en they were youngsters
White Lodge, Richmond.
y planned one day to star
he Royal Opera House, Covent Garden,
ere you see a dream come true.

Alfreda in a
typical arabesque.

ured here are scenes from "In the Beginning"
xciting and arresting ballet
d on a classical technique.
motif of the rising sun strikes a strange note
gives the ballet a dramatic impact.

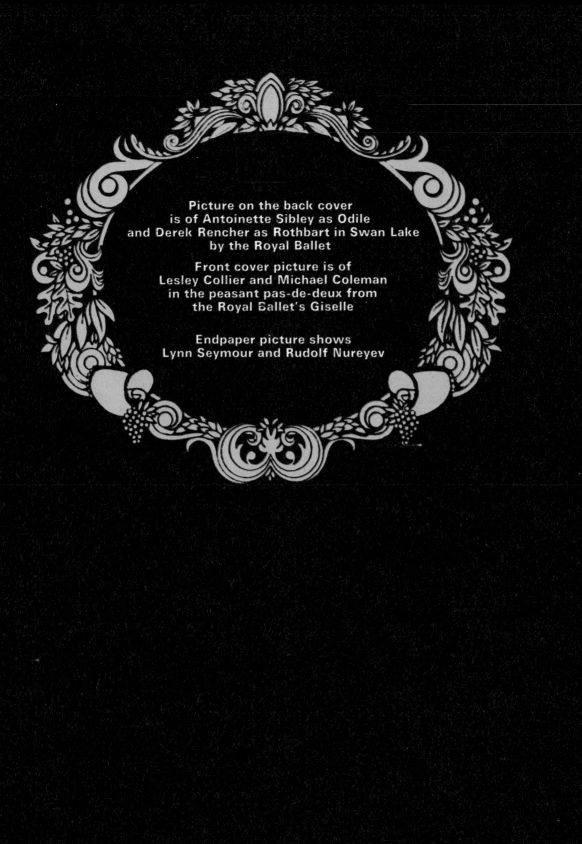

Picture on the back cover
is of Antoinette Sibley as Odile
and Derek Rencher as Rothbart in Swan Lake
by the Royal Ballet

Front cover picture is of
Lesley Collier and Michael Coleman
in the peasant pas-de-deux from
the Royal Ballet's Giselle

Endpaper picture shows
Lynn Seymour and Rudolf Nureyev